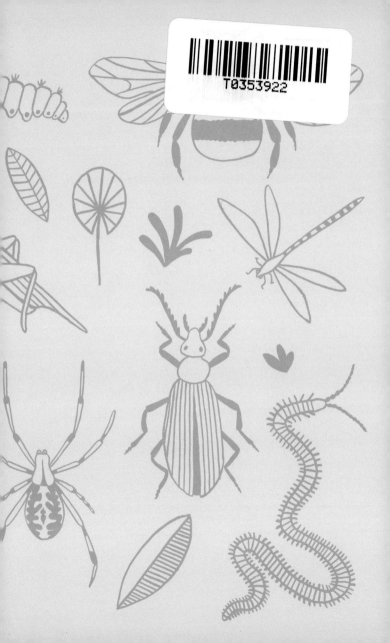

T0353922

SERIES 208

In this book we will examine some of the smallest creepy-crawlies – from transforming caterpillars and architect arachnids to bodybuilding ants and industrious bees.

LADYBIRD BOOKS

UK | USA | Canada | Ireland | Australia
India | New Zealand | South Africa

Ladybird Books is part of the Penguin Random House group of companies
whose addresses can be found at global.penguinrandomhouse.com

www.penguin.co.uk   www.puffin.co.uk   www.ladybird.co.uk.

Penguin
Random House
UK

First published 2020

001

Copyright © Ladybird Books Ltd, 2020

Printed in China

A CIP catalogue record for this book is available from the British Library

ISBN: 978-0-241-41703-4

All correspondence to:

Ladybird Books
Penguin Random House Children's
One Embassy Gardens, New Union Square
5 Nine Elms Lane, London SW8 5DA

Insects and Minibeasts

A Ladybird Book

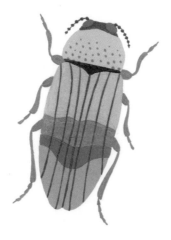

Written by Libby Walden
with entomological consultant, Heather Campbell

Illustrated by Amber Davenport

Minibeasts vs. insects

Minibeast is a general term that means "small creature" and can include anything from ants and slugs to beetles and spiders. Minibeasts can look incredibly different and live in completely different environments, but they all have one thing in common — minibeasts do not have a backbone or internal skeleton so they are known as "invertebrates".

Ninety-six per cent of all animals are invertebrates. This enormous category is broken up into smaller classes and families. Slugs and snails are molluscs, spiders, mites and ticks are arachnids and the woodlouse is a crustacean. But the largest of the groups is the insects. Scientists have discovered over a million different species of insect, and they are sure there are more to find . . .

A true insect has two feelers, or "antennae", on its head, its body is divided into three parts — the head, the thorax (middle) and the abdomen — and it must have three pairs of jointed legs coming from its thorax. According to the rules of the animal kingdom, it is true to say that all insects are minibeasts, but not all minibeasts are insects!

1. Orchid bee
2. Woodlouse
3. Earthworm
4. Orb-weaver spider
5. Leopard slug
6. Cardinal beetle
7. Leech
8. Wasp
9. Black ant
10. Katydid
11. Cuban land snail

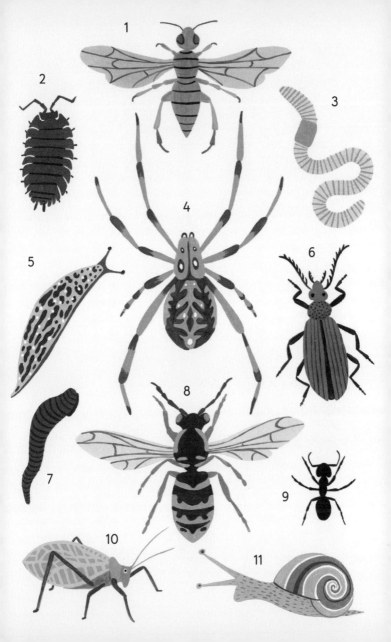

Ant

Ants are social insects that live in large, organized groups known as "colonies". In the year 2000, an enormous colony of ants was found in southern Europe. This Argentine-ant supercolony stretched over 3,700 miles (6,000 km) wide and contained millions of nests and billions of workers!

Ant colonies vary in size, but each one usually serves a single queen. The queen is often a lot larger than the other ants and is the only female able to lay eggs. The other female ants are known as the "workers". They perform as a team, working together to build structures, find food, look after the young and defend their nest from attackers.

Leafcutter ants are famous for their strength. A single ant is able to carry over 50 times its own body weight. They use their powerful jaws to tear away large pieces of leaf and carry them back to the nest. Leafcutters work as a team, travelling through the forest in lines that can stretch up to 75 metres (246 ft) in length.

As ants don't have ears, they communicate in non-verbal ways. If danger or a food source has been found, ants release chemical signals, called "pheromones", to alert each other. They can also sense vibrations through their feet and touch antennae to send messages.

Beetle

More than one third of all insects are beetles. There are around 400,000 named species of beetle, and they can be found in mountainous regions, deserts, woodlands and wetlands. They also come in all shapes, sizes and colours.

Poo-loving dung beetles have two distinct ways of collecting and transporting manure. Some dung beetles create poo balls that they roll along the ground. Others bury their poo stash in the ground. A third group choose to live in the manure rather than move it anywhere!

The ground bombardier beetle has a rather dramatic way of getting rid of predators. They store two chemicals in their bodies, which, when combined, cause a hot, toxic spray to jet out in all directions.

Wood-boring jewel beetles are known for their shiny, multi-coloured wing cases, known as "elytra". In the past, humans harvested these wing cases to make jewellery, textiles and beetle-wing embroidery.

The impressive mandibles, or "mouthpieces", of the male stag beetles look similar to the antlers of a deer, which is where their name comes from. Male stag beetles use their curved jaws to fight and wrestle with each other over food and female beetles.

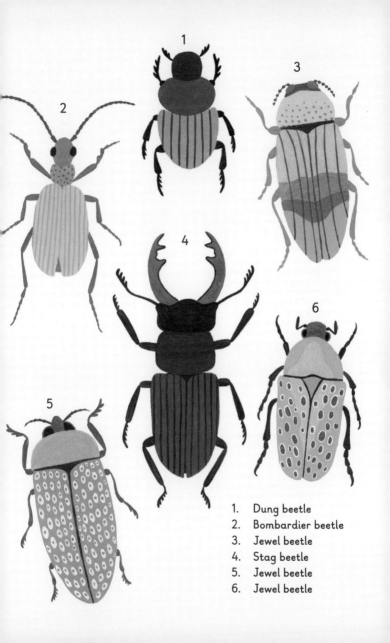

1. Dung beetle
2. Bombardier beetle
3. Jewel beetle
4. Stag beetle
5. Jewel beetle
6. Jewel beetle

Ladybird

One of the most familiar beetles is the ladybird. Also known as "ladybug", "lady cow", "lady fly" or "lady beetle", this small, dome-shaped beetle is loved by gardeners as it feasts on aphids – sap-sucking insects that can destroy plants and crops.

Ranging from 0.8 millimetre (0.03 in.) to 18 millimetres (0.7 in.) in size, ladybirds are known for their brightly coloured wing cases, or "elytra". The most well-known ladybird species has bright red elytra with black spots, but others are yellow, orange or brown with white or red spots. Some ladybirds have even swapped their spots for stripes!

The ladybird's striking appearance is used as a defence. The bright red warns predators that the beetle could taste very bitter if eaten. If the predator chooses to ignore this warning, and picks up or disturbs the ladybird, this beetle will then produce a smelly, oily liquid from their leg joints.

People used to think that the number of spots on the back of a ladybird showed its age (for example, one spot = one year). In fact, for most ladybirds, the number of spots relates to its species. For example, the two-spotted ladybird and the larger seven-spotted ladybird are both found in Europe.

Land snail

All land snails are gastropod molluscs. Molluscs are part of the animal family of invertebrates, which also includes squid, clams and octopuses. Gastropod is a term that comes from Greek and means "stomach foot". As molluscs, snails have soft bodies with no skeleton, but they do have protection in the form of a shell.

Snail shells are made from a material called "calcium carbonate". Snails are born with their shells and, as they grow older, they produce new layers of shell to make sure their protective casing grows with them. The layers of calcium carbonate create the spiral shape we often see on the shells of land snails.

Depending on the species, land snails can travel at a speed between 1 millimetre (0.04 in.) and 18 millimetres (0.7 in.) per second – they are very slow-moving creatures! Snails travel on a single, muscular foot, which moves in waves across the ground.

To move safely across lots of different terrains, snails produce slime called "mucus", which gives them a slicker surface to glide along. This mucus is so effective that a snail could travel over something as fine as a needle point without any injury.

Slug

Like snails, slugs are also gastropod molluscs, but they do not carry a shell as snails do. Instead, most slug species have a plate beneath their skin that helps to protect them. This plate sits next to the fleshy area behind the head, known as the "mantle" or "saddle".

Temperature is very important to slugs. They spend most of their time underground, feasting on roots and seeds. When the ground temperature heats up to over 5 degrees Celsius, slugs become more active and venture above the surface. Slugs particularly enjoy damp conditions and are often spotted in the wild after heavy rainfall.

Climate also affects the development of slug eggs. Slugs reproduce a few times each year, laying between 20 and 100 eggs at a time. The jelly-like, watery eggs develop faster in warmer temperatures, and slugs can take up to a year to become a fully grown adult.

To keep healthy, adult slugs eat up to 40 times their own body weight in food a day! They chew through plant matter using a tongue-like organ called a "radula". The radula is covered in thousands of "denticles" or tiny teeth!

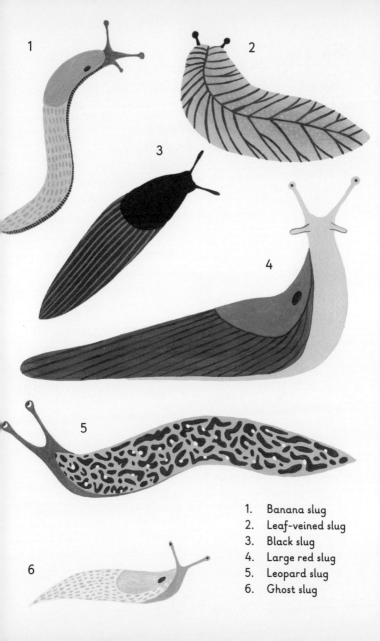

1. Banana slug
2. Leaf-veined slug
3. Black slug
4. Large red slug
5. Leopard slug
6. Ghost slug

Fly

There are a lot of flying insects with "-fly" at the end of their name – butterfly, dragonfly, damselfly, and so on – but these are not "true" flies. True flies have a single pair of wings with a tiny stabilizer, or "haltere", set behind each wing.

A haltere is a small, knobbly bump that moves in the opposite direction to the wing, counterbalancing the wing's movement like a seesaw. Halteres act like stabilizers on a bicycle, helping the fly to remain steady in the air, especially when it performs acrobatic movements. Flies can travel forwards, backwards and from side to side with ease.

Flies look at the world in a very different way to humans. They have compound eyes, which are fixed in one place and made up of thousands of tiny little lenses. The round shape, multi-lens structure and slightly raised position of the eyes give the fly an almost 360-degree view of the world.

The way a fly's eyes work means that they do not see as clearly as humans. They see their surroundings in thousands of small broken-up pieces. The benefit of this is that they are incredibly sensitive to any change in light or movement, such as that caused by a predator approaching, and can fly off before getting caught.

Spider

There are around 40,000 recorded species of spider in the world, and spiders are believed to have existed for more than 320 million years. These eight-legged invertebrates have two main body parts – the head and thorax, and the abdomen. Most spiders also have fine hairs covering their casing, or "exoskeleton". These help the spider to taste and feel the air and grip onto smoother surfaces.

Half of all spider species are considered to be architects. They create silk proteins in their abdomen and use special spinnerets to build webs and hideouts to catch their prey, which can be anything from a fly to a small bird. As the liquid silk protein leaves the spider's spinnerets, it hardens into strands and creates a sticky net for prey.

Spiderwebs come in many different designs, from pizza-slice triangles to veil-like sheets across tree branches. Each web is different and varies in style and strength depending on the species of spider that has built it.

Webs that look like a bicycle wheel are known as "orb webs". Orb-weaver spiders will build the main structure and shape of the web before adding in connecting sticky spiral threads. Some orb-weavers add features to strengthen the web. For example, the wasp spider weaves an extra band of silk down the centre of its web in a zigzag pattern.

Grasshopper and cricket

Grasshoppers and crickets belong to the same order of insects and can be found in similar habitats, preferring warm weather and dry environments. They also have similar body shapes – squat, long bodies with large hind legs and antennae. But there are also a few differences.

Grasshoppers are often larger than crickets, with some species reaching 10 centimetres (4 in.) in length. The largest species of cricket only grows to about 5 centimetres (2 in.), but crickets often have longer antennae. Crickets are also more active at night and so have a darker casing, or "exoskeleton", than the green or brown grasshoppers.

Most species of cricket, whether they have wings or not, move by hopping or jumping. However, a grasshopper will use its large back legs to catapult itself into the air. Grasshoppers can leap up to 20 times the length of their own bodies and, once airborne, they are also able to fly.

To attract a female, the male cricket will rub its wings together to create a loud chirping noise. This is called "stridulating" and is often heard during the summer months. Only a few species of grasshopper can make a noise that humans are able to hear, but both male and female grasshoppers are able to make music. They rub their hind legs against their wings to create soft, muffled sounds.

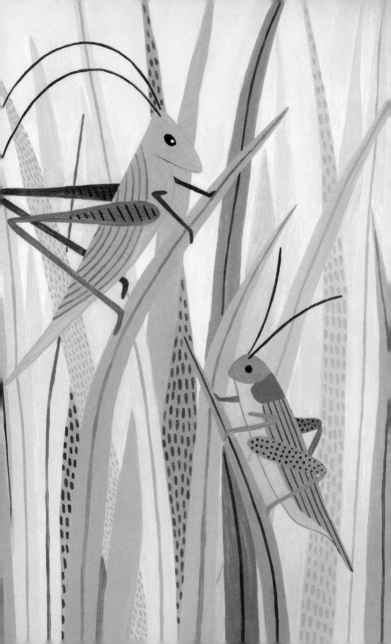

Bee

Bees are flying insects that are famous for producing honey and beeswax, and for collecting pollen and nectar from flowers. Bees are able to beat their wings around 11,400 times per minute. This not only makes them effective fliers but also creates their famous buzz.

Honeybees live in large groups called "colonies", each containing a single queen, male drones and female worker bees. Each bee has a role. The queen lays eggs as the male drones fertilize them. The female workers do a variety of jobs, including gathering pollen, feeding larvae, cleaning the hive or guarding the queen.

The largest and fluffiest species of bee is the bumblebee. Its size means it creates more heat, so bumblebees can survive in cooler weather than other bee species. As they harvest nectar and pollen from flowering plants, bumblebees mark the flowers they have visited with a scent so they don't make the mistake of revisiting empty blooms.

Unlike honeybees and bumblebees, the solitary bee lives alone. As they do not produce honey or serve a queen, every female solitary bee is able to lay eggs. The female will create individual cells in which she lays an egg and places some pollen for the larvae to eat once it hatches. She will then seal off the entrance and start again.

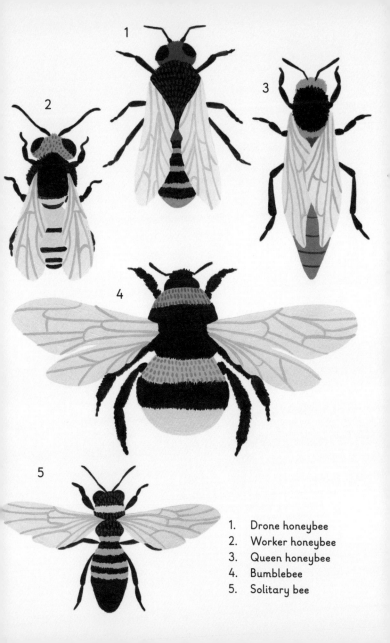

1. Drone honeybee
2. Worker honeybee
3. Queen honeybee
4. Bumblebee
5. Solitary bee

The honeybee hive

Wild honeybees create shelters, or hives, in tree trunks, on branches or between rocks. The hive houses a bee colony – a group of bees made up of a queen, hundreds of male drones and thousands of female workers. The size of a colony can vary between 10,000 and 60,000 bees.

The location of a beehive is very important. As a large number of worker bees are sent to find nectar, water, tree sap and pollen, the closer the hive is to flowers and plants, the less flying the workers have to do. Bees will travel up to 5 miles (8 km) in search of food, but the average journey is usually 0.5 to 2 miles (0.8 to 3.2 km).

Hives are made using a special wax, known as "beeswax". When honeybees are around ten days old, they develop a wax-producing gland, which can change the sugar in honey into a waxy material. The small flakes of wax are then gathered and chewed by other bees to mould into cells of honeycomb.

The hexagonal shape of a honeycomb cell is an important design feature. These six-sided tubes require the least amount of wax to build, but they hold the most honey. Cells are used to house bee larvae and stores of honey or pollen.

Earthworm

Earthworms are tube-shaped, segmented worms that mostly live underground. In general, earthworms are very sensitive to light and must keep their skin moist in order to breathe. This means that earthworms often only visit the surface at night or, for certain species, to find food or to mate.

As they don't have arms or legs, earthworms move through the earth by lengthening and shortening their muscles to create a wave, which then moves their body forward. An earthworm's skin produces mucus to help it slip through the soil, and each segment of an earthworm's body is covered in tiny bristle-like hairs called "setae" that add grip.

Earthworms are often called the gardener's or the farmer's "best friend". This is because, as they travel through the earth, the earthworms improve the quality of the soil. The tunnels created by the worms allow water and air to move through the ground more easily. This helps plants to access these two vital things more readily and, as a result, the plants will be healthier and will grow better.

Earthworms are also decomposers. This means they eat decaying animal and plant matter, such as roots and leaves. As they digest their food, the vital nutrients and minerals in the organic matter break down and are returned to the soil through the earthworms' poo.

Caterpillar

The caterpillar is both an insect and the offspring, or "larva", of a butterfly or moth. They come in all shapes and sizes and can be brightly coloured, hairy, patterned or plain. A caterpillar's appearance varies between species and is related to the environment in which it lives.

After a caterpillar has hatched from its egg, its sole purpose is to eat. Some caterpillars will even shed their skin up to five times because they grow so quickly. If they didn't shed their old skin, they would burst out of it! Almost all caterpillars are plant eaters, or "herbivores", but there are a few that feed on small insects, and even other caterpillars.

Caterpillars can eat up to 1,000 times their body weight in preparation for their next phase of growth. This is called the "pupa stage". Once a caterpillar is ready, it will develop a hard outer case (known as a "chrysalis") or weave a silk sleeping bag called a "cocoon". This will protect the caterpillar as it turns into a butterfly or a moth. This process is called "metamorphosis".

Once wrapped inside its new shell, the caterpillar will use its digestive juices to dissolve most of its old body. Depending on the species, it can take the caterpillar anywhere from a few days to a year to reach its final, adult stage, when it will break out of its chrysalis or cocoon as a butterfly or moth.

1. Eggs
2. Caterpillar
3. Chrysalis
4. Butterfly

Butterfly

There are roughly 18,500 different species of butterfly dotted around the globe. Butterflies exist on every continent except Antarctica. Adult butterflies have liquid diets, mostly surviving on a mix of water and flower nectar, although some species will eat tree sap, rotting fruit and the minerals found in mud and sand.

The butterfly's most striking feature is its four wings. Often brightly coloured with spots or patterns, a butterfly uses its wings to fly, to attract a mate or to blend into its habitat.

When a caterpillar transforms into a butterfly within a chrysalis, its wings develop around its body. Once the butterfly is fully formed and breaks free of the chrysalis, its wings appear as limp, wet tissue. Body fluid is then pumped into the veins in the wings, which helps to straighten them out. The butterfly will rest during this time as its wings need to harden and dry before it can take flight.

Despite the beautiful colours, butterfly wings are actually see-through. Each wing is covered in thousands of tiny scales that reflect light. This creates the colours and patterns that humans see. Underneath the scales, the wings are actually made of very thin, see-through layers. As a butterfly ages, its scales sometimes fall off to reveal transparent spots where the protein layer is uncovered.

1. Monarch butterfly
2. Eighty-eight butterfly
3. Blue morpho butterfly
4. Peacock butterfly
5. Cabbage white butterfly
6. Buckeye butterfly

Dragonfly

They may have a romantic name, but dragonflies are actually skilled and ferocious hunters. In flight, these insects are able to judge the speed and direction of other flying insects, such as gnats and mosquitoes. Much like a radio-controlled torpedo, a dragonfly will then lock on to its prey and target it with sharp focus and precision before going in for the kill.

The dragonfly has superior flying skills to aid it in its hunt. Dragonflies can work their two sets of wings independently from each other, using special muscles at the base of the wing, in the thorax. This allows the insect to change the angle of each wing and perform complicated flying moves, including flying straight up and down, hovering like a helicopter and speeding through the air at up to 25 to 30 miles (40 to 48 km) per hour.

Most species of dragonfly will even lay eggs while in flight. The dragonfly will hover over the surface of a water source, dip the end of its abdomen below the water line and release eggs. These jelly-covered eggs will either drift on the surface before eventually sticking to water plants or sink to the bottom until they are ready to hatch. Dragonfly larvae will then live underwater for up to two years before rising to the surface and taking flight.

Centipede and millipede

Centipedes and millipedes are grouped together into a category of animals known as "myriapods". Like insects, these creepy-crawlies have a tough exoskeleton and a pair of antennae, or "feelers", growing from their head. However, centipedes and millipedes are set apart by the number of jointed legs they have.

As "centi-" comes from the Latin meaning "hundred" and "milli-" means "thousand", it is often assumed that these many-legged creatures have a hundred or a thousand legs. Unfortunately, it is not quite that simple. Centipedes can travel on fourteen to 177 pairs of legs, whereas millipedes have roughly 200 pairs. One specimen of the *Illacme plenipes* millipede has been recorded as having 750 legs (but that's still not quite 1,000!).

Centipedes prefer to live in damp environments – under rocks, in soil and in decaying leaf litter. Unlike other insects, the centipede's flattened exoskeleton is not waxy and so these myriapods need to live in a moist habitat to stay alive.

The exoskeletons of most millipedes look like armoured plates. Instead of biting when attacked, a millipede will curl up into a coil or ball, so that only their plates are on show. This protects their softer underside as well as making them bulky, so they are much harder to carry or swallow.

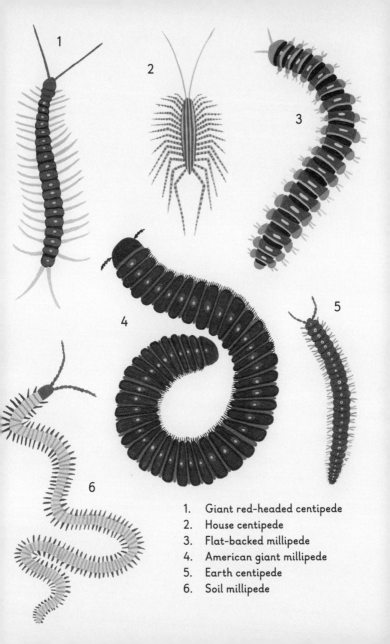

1. Giant red-headed centipede
2. House centipede
3. Flat-backed millipede
4. American giant millipede
5. Earth centipede
6. Soil millipede

Praying mantis

There are over 2,400 species of mantis living in tropical and mild, or "temperate", habitats around the world. These insects have large, triangular heads with two multi-lens compound eyes, three other "simple" eyes and a sharp, beak-like mouthpiece.

The common term "praying mantis" is used for all species of mantis, although it is most often related to the European *Mantis religiosa*. The name comes from the position of the mantis's front legs. All species have folded-over forelegs, making the insect look like it is praying.

A mantis's forelegs are very important when it comes to hunting. Adult females are usually too large to fly and so they rely on their 180-degree vision and their lightning-quick reflexes to catch prey. Their front forelegs can move incredibly fast, grabbing live prey before it has even noticed that the mantis has moved.

Praying mantises are meat-eating, or "carnivorous", insects. Mantises live on a diet of spiders, grasshoppers, small frogs and lizards, crickets and even other praying mantises. They may be vicious hunters, but the mantis's table manners are flawless, as it cleans its forelegs after every meal.

Important insects

In spite of their size, insects, minibeasts and creepy-crawlies are incredibly important. They are pollinators, recyclers and tasty snacks and without insects, humans would be lost.

Bees and other flying insects are crucial for the survival of some plant species. As they visit flowers to feed on nectar, these insects accidentally collect pollen on their legs and bodies. They will then take this pollen to other blooms, which fertilizes the new flower's egg cells. These cells then grow into seeds, often surrounded by berries or fruit. Without insects, this process of fertilization, or "pollination", would not happen.

Decomposer insects help to speed up the breakdown of plant matter and other organic waste products. By eating dead wood and decaying leaves, insects like beetles, earthworms and flies help to recycle the nutrients and return them to the soil, ready for new plants to grow.

Minibeasts are a great source of protein. As a readily available, sustainable and rich food source, insects keep a lot of creatures on the go – including around two billion humans! Scientists predict that insects will become a more popular food for humans in the future as a way to feed growing populations and reduce the amount of meat and fish currently on the menu.

Protecting insects

Pollution levels, loss of natural areas (known as "habitats"), climate change and the use of chemicals in farming all threaten insect life. But what can humans do to help? Here are a few small ways that might make a big difference.

Like humans, insects need to be near a source of fresh water so that they can drink and stay refreshed. Putting out a bowl of water, topping up a birdbath or making sure a garden pond is clean all help to keep water sources readily available to insects.

Building a bug hotel from natural materials, like straw and wood, provides a multistorey home for many creatures and creepy crawlies. These hotels can shelter hedgehogs and toads as well as solitary bees, ladybirds, woodlice and butterflies.

Try to make gardens, patios and balconies as insect-friendly as they can be. Evergreen shrubs will attract woodlice and spiders. Meadow-like patches or pots of wildflowers will provide food and shelter to a whole variety of insects, including bees and butterflies.

A Ladybird Book

collectable books for curious kids

What to Look For in Spring

9780241416181

What to Look For in Summer

9780241416204

What to Look For in Autumn

9780241416167

What to Look For in Winter

9780241416228

SERIES 205